What Is HOMOPHOBIA?

AJ Knight

 Explore other books at:
WWW.ENGAGEBOOKS.COM

VANCOUVER, B.C.

 WWW.ENGAGEBOOKS.COM

What Is Homophobia? -
Working Towards Equality: Level 3
Knight, AJ –
Text © 2023 Engage Books
Design © 2023 Engage Books

Edited by: A.R. Roumanis, Ashley Lee, and Melody Sun
Design by: Mandy Christiansen

Text set in Montserrat Regular.
Chapter headings set in Merlo Neue.

If you are part of the LGBTQ+ community and are thinking of harming yourself, contact The Trevor Project for help. Text "START" to 678-678, call 1-866-488-7386, or chat online at thetrevorproject.org/get-help

FIRST EDITION / FIRST PRINTING

All rights reserved. No part of this book may be stored in a retrieval system, reproduced or transmitted in any form or by any other means without written permission from the publisher or a licence from the Canadian Copyright Licensing Agency. Critics and reviewers may quote brief passages in connection with a review or critical article in any media.

Every reasonable effort has been made to contact the copyright holders of all material reproduced in this book.

LIBRARY AND ARCHIVES CANADA CATALOGUING IN PUBLICATION

Title: What is homophobia? / AJ Knight.
Names: Knight, AJ, author.
Description: Series statement: Working towards equality

Identifiers: Canadiana (print) 20230447600 | Canadiana (ebook) 20230447619
ISBN 978-1-77476-859-4 (hardcover)
ISBN 978-1-77476-860-0 (softcover)
ISBN 978-1-77476-861-7 (epub)
ISBN 978-1-77476-862-4 (pdf)
ISBN 978-1-77878-130-8 (audio)

Subjects:
LCSH: Homophobia—Juvenile literature.
LCSH: Transphobia—Juvenile literature.

Classification: LCC HQ76.4 .K65 2023 | DDC J306.76—DC23

This project has been made possible in part by the Government of Canada.

Contents

- 4   What Is Homosexuality?
- 6   What Is Homophobia?
- 8   Why Do People Have Different Sexual Orientations?
- 10   The History of Homophobia 1
- 12   The History of Homophobia 2
- 14   Why Are Some People Homophobic?
- 16   What Does Homophobia Look Like?
- 18   What to Do if You Experience Homophobia 1
- 20   What to Do if You Experience Homophobia 2
- 22   Equality Superheroes in the Past
- 24   Equality Superheroes Today
- 26   Ways to Support Change 1 and 2
- 28   Ways to Support Change 3 and 4
- 30   Quiz

What Is Homosexuality?

Homosexuality describes people who are **attracted** to people of the same gender. Gender is a person's inner sense of whether they are a boy, girl, or something else. Today, it is more common to use the words "lesbian" or "gay" instead of homosexual.

KEY WORD

Attracted: strongly liking someone or something.

Women who are attracted to other women are called "lesbian." Men who are attracted to other men are called "gay." People who are attracted to more than one gender are called "bisexual."

"Gay" is a term that is often used to describe anyone who feels attracted to the same gender.

What Is Homophobia?

Homophobia is when someone is treated poorly because they feel same-sex attraction. Both **heterosexual** and gay people can be homophobic. Homophobia comes from the idea that everyone should be heterosexual.

KEY WORD

Heterosexual: someone who is attracted to people of the opposite gender. They are also called "straight."

The word "homophobia" does not perfectly describe what it actually is. Phobias are things that cause fear or worry. Homophobic behavior often comes from feelings of **disgust**. But it can come from feelings of fear as well.

KEY WORD

Disgust: a strong feeling of not liking someone or something.

Why Do People Have Different Sexual Orientations?

No one knows why people have different **sexual orientations**. Someone's sexual orientation may change over time. But no one can force sexual orientation to change.

> **KEY WORD**
>
> **Sexual orientations:** ways of describing the gender or genders someone is attracted to.

Using words like "gay" and "lesbian" can help people find community. A community is a group of people who have something in common. Gay people are part of the LGBTQ+ community. This is a group of people with **diverse** genders and sexual orientations.

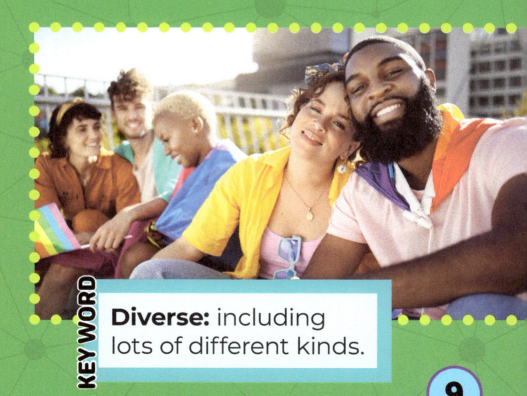

KEY WORD

Diverse: including lots of different kinds.

The History of Homophobia 1

Homophobia has been around for a very long time. Laws making homosexuality a crime were created near the end of Ancient Rome. These laws were eventually used to create homophobic laws in Europe and North America.

As of 2023, it was still a crime to be gay in about 64 countries worldwide.

In 1553, King Henry VIII of England made it a crime to be gay. People who felt same-sex attraction were put to death. The law changed in 1861. Instead of being put to death, people were put in jail for 10 years or longer.

The History of Homophobia 2

Dr. George Weinberg first used the word "homophobia" in the 1960s. He noticed that other people's fear of gay people also made them feel disgust and anger. Dr. Weinberg later helped get homosexuality taken off the list of mental illnesses in the United States.

On June 28, 1969, police tried to arrest people for being homosexual at a **gay bar** called the Stonewall Inn in New York. The people of Stonewall fought back for many days. This event was called the Stonewall Uprising.

KEY WORD

Gay bar: a place where adults from the LGBTQ+ community can get together and feel safe.

Why Are Some People Homophobic?

No one is born homophobic. Someone might learn to be homophobic from their family or friends. They might see homophobic behavior on TV. Some people are homophobic because it makes them feel powerful.

Internalized homophobia is when someone accepts the homophobic beliefs they have been taught. Anyone can have internalized homophobia. Gay people with internalized homophobia often have a hard time admitting their feelings.

What Does Homophobia Look Like?

Laws that make homosexuality a crime are homophobic. Hurting someone because they are gay is also homophobic. It is homophobic to not give someone else a job because of their sexual orientation.

Homophobia can be hard to spot in everyday life. Here are some homophobic behaviors.

1. Name-calling.
2. Not wanting to hug gay people.
3. Making jokes about gay people.
4. Refusing to believe someone's sexuality.
5. Assuming that someone is straight.
6. Saying that someone does not look gay.
7. Calling someone's romantic partner their friend.

What to Do if You Experience Homophobia 1

Your safety is more important than anything else. If you are in danger, stay calm, go to a safe place, and get help. Homophobia is never okay, no matter who it comes from.

Save any homophobic messages you get online to show an adult.

Tell a teacher or parent if you can. If you are not comfortable telling a parent or teacher, find another trusted adult. Write down the homophobic behavior or words to show an adult.

What to Do if You Experience Homophobia 2

Talk to a trusted friend about what happened. Join a local LGBTQ+ community if you can. Gay Straight Alliances (GSAs) are school clubs for students who are LGBTQ+ and those who support them. GSAs create safe spaces for people to be themselves.

Talking about homophobia you have experienced can be scary. Connecting with others can give you comfort and support. If you do not have anyone to talk to, reading books with gay characters can help you feel more connected to the gay community.

Equality Superheroes in the Past

Marsha P. Johnson was a **transgender** woman known for helping with the 1960s–1970s gay rights movement. She fought for gay and transgender rights and LGBTQ+ people affected by homelessness. Marsha is well-known for joining the Stonewall Uprising.

KEY WORD

Transgender: someone whose gender is different from the one they were given at birth.

Edith Windsor was a gay rights activist and lesbian woman. An activist is someone who fights for positive changes in the world. Edith is known for fighting back when the US government would not accept her marriage. Her fight led to more rights for homosexual couples.

Bayard Rustin fought for the rights of many different people. He was put in jail in 1953 for being gay. Bayard began speaking out for gay and lesbian rights in the 1970s.

Equality Superheroes Today

Daniel Radcliffe is an actor who speaks out about gay rights. For years, he has supported a group that helps LGBTQ+ people called The Trevor Project. Daniel has recorded videos with The Trevor Project in support of gay and transgender people and was given the Trevor Hero Award.

Billie Jean King is a tennis player and an activist for gay and women's rights. She has been openly lesbian since the 1980s. Billie has raised money to fight homophobia in schools and to prevent the deaths of gay people.

Menaka Guruswamy is a lawyer who has fought hard for the LGBTQ+ community in India. In 2018, she helped get rid of a law that made being gay a crime. Getting rid of this law also meant gay people in India got more rights.

Ways to Support Change 1

Take time to educate yourself about the experiences of gay people. Read books with gay characters, and listen when people share their stories. Do not assume that someone is straight.

Treat your LGBTQ+ friends how you want to be treated. Include them in games and invite them to hang out. Listen respectfully if they open up to you about something.

Ways to Support Change 2

Use **inclusive** language that respects people of all sexual orientations and genders. Avoid using hurtful terms about someone's sexual orientation. By using inclusive language, you can help everyone feel more comfortable.

KEY WORD

Inclusive: leaving no one out.

The first pride parade was celebrated one year after the Stonewall Uprising.

Attend a pride parade. These are events that celebrate the LGBTQ+ community and remind people about the Stonewall Uprising. Different parts of the world celebrate pride on different days. Look online to find out when pride happens where you live.

Quiz

Test your knowledge of homophobia by answering the following questions. The questions are based on what you have read in this book. The answers are listed on the bottom of the next page.

1 What is a term that is often used to describe anyone who feels attracted to the same gender?

2 What is homophobia?

3 What is a community?

4 Who helped get homosexuality taken off the list of mental illnesses in the United States?

5 Are people born homophobic?

6 What are pride parades?

30

Explore Other Level 3 Readers.

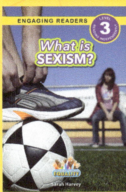

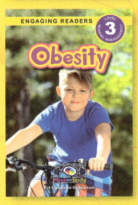

Visit www.engagebooks.com/readers

Answers: 1. Gay 2. When someone is treated poorly because they feel same-sex attraction 3. A group of people who have something in common 4. Dr. George Weinberg 5. No 6. Events that celebrate the LGBTQ+ community and remind people about the Stonewall Uprising

Milton Keynes UK
Ingram Content Group UK Ltd.
UKHW022232180823
427115UK00009B/44

What Is HOMOPHOBIA?

It's likely that you have already witnessed homophobia. The hatred and prejudice directed at people within the LGBTQ+ community is hard to miss. Learn how to spot homophobic language and behavior. Become an ally. It is a powerful thing to do in the face of hate.

Level 3 readers are aimed at children who are reading by themselves and can grasp new concepts. Key words and captions help readers understand new vocabulary and more challenging sentence structure.

Explore other Level 3 readers!

 Beginner reader

 Reading together

 Reading with help

Reading independently

This project has been made possible in part by the Government of Canada.

Cover design: A.R. Roumanis

ISBN 978-1-77476-860-0

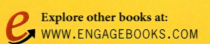

Explore other books at:
WWW.ENGAGEBOOKS.COM